sundance™

LITTLE RED
READERS

In the Sea

PETER SLOAN &
SHERYL SLOAN

A whale lives
in the sea.

A dolphin lives
in the sea.

A shark lives
in the sea.

A stingray lives
in the sea.

A lobster lives
in the sea.

A giant turtle lives
in the sea.

An octopus lives
in the sea.